P9-AOI-278

WITHDRAWN

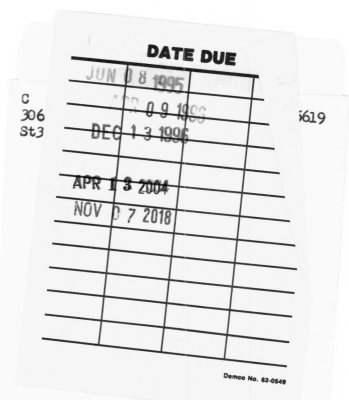

**DATE DUE**

| | | |
|---|---|---|
| JUN 0 8 1995 | | |
| APR 0 9 1996 | | |
| DEC 1 3 1996 | | |
| | | |
| APR 1 3 2004 | | |
| NOV 0 7 2018 | | |
| | | |
| | | |
| | | |
| | | |

Demco No. 62-0549

C
306
St3

5619

# ON DIVORCE

Library of Congress Cataloging in Publication Data

Stein, Sara Bonnett.
  On divorce.

  (An open family book)
  SUMMARY: Separate text for parents and children
explore various emotions aroused by divorce.
    1.  Divorce—United States—Juvenile literature.
[1. Divorce]  I. Stone, Erika.  II. Title.
HQ834.S73  1979     301.42'84     78-19687
ISBN 0-8027-6344-8

Text Copyright © 1979 by Sara Bonnett Stein
Photographs Copyright © 1979 by Erika Stone

All rights reserved. No part of this book may be
reproduced or transmitted in any form or by any
means, electronic or mechanical, including
photocopying, recording, or by any information
storage and retrieval system, without permission
in writing from the Publisher.

First published in the United States of America in
1979 by the Walker Publishing Company, Inc.

Published simultaneously in Canada by Beaver-
books, Limited, Pickering, Ontario

ISBN 0-8027-6344-8

Library of Congress Catalog Card Number
78-19687

Printed in the United States of America

# ON DIVORCE

## An Open Family Book For Parents And Children Together

by Sara Bonnett Stein

Thomas R. Holman,
Ph.D., Consultant
Psychologist, Postgraduate Center
for Mental Health, New York, New York

Photographs by Erika Stone

145619

CODY MEMORIAL LIBRARY
SOUTHWESTERN UNIVERSITY
GEORGETOWN, TEXAS

Walker and Company
New York, New York
Created by Media Projects Incorporated

# A Note About This Book

When your child was a baby, you took him to the doctor to have him immunized for childhood illnesses. The injections hurt a little, but you knew they would prepare his body to cope with far more serious threats in the future. Yet there are other threats as painful and destructive to a child's growth as physical illness: separation from his parents, a death in the family, a new baby, fears and fantasies of his own imagining that hurt as much as pain itself. These Open Family Books are to help adults prepare children for common hurts of childhood.

Caring adults try to protect their child from difficult events. But still that child has ears that overhear, eyes that read the faces of adults around him. If people are sad, he knows it. If people are worried, he knows it. If people are angry, he knows that too.

What he doesn't know—if no one tells him—is the whole story. In his attempts to make sense of what is going on around him, he fills in the fragments he has noticed with fantasied explanations of his own which, because he is a child, are often more frightening than the truth.

We protect children because we know them to be different, more easily damaged than ourselves. But the difference we sense is not widely understood. Children are more easily damaged because they cannot make distinctions yet between what is real and what is unreal, what is magic and what is logic. The tiger under a child's bed at night is as real to him as the tiger in the zoo. When he wishes a bad thing, he believes his wish can make the bad thing happen. His fearful imagining about what is going on grips him because he has no way to test the truth of it.

It is the job of parents to support and explain reality, to guide a child toward the truth even if it is painful. The dose may be small, just as a dose of vaccine is adjusted to the smallness of a baby; but even if it is a little at a time, it is only straightforwardness that gives children the internal strength to deal with things not as they imagine them to be, but as they are.

To do that, parents need to understand what sorts of fears, fantasies, misunderstandings are common to early childhood—what they might expect at three years old, or at five, or seven. They need simpler ways to explain the way complicated things are. The adult text of each of these books, in

306.89
+340

the left-hand column, explains extraordinary ways that ordinary children between three and eight years old attempt to make sense of difficult events in their lives. It puts into words uncomplicated ways to say things. It is probably best to read the adult text several times before you read the book to your child, so you will get a comfortable feel for the ideas and so you won't be distracted as you talk together. If your child can read, he may one day be curious to read the adult text. That's all right. What's written there is the same as what you are talking about together. The pictures and the words in large print are to start the talking between you and your child. The stories are intense enough to arouse curiosity and feeling. But they are reasonable, forthright and gentle, so a child can deal with the material at whatever level he is ready for.

The themes in these Open Family Books are common to children's play. That is no accident. Play, joyous but also serious, is the way a child enacts himself a little bit at a time, to get used to events, thoughts and feelings he is confused about. Helping a child keep clear on the difference between what is real and what is fantasy will not restrict a child's creativity in play. It will let him use fantasy more freely because it is less frightening.

In some ways, these books won't work. No matter how a parent explains things, a child will misunderstand some part of the explanation, sometimes right away, sometimes in retrospect, weeks or even months later. Parents really can't help this fact of psychological life. Nothing in human growing works all at once, completely or forever. But parents can keep the channels of communication open so that gradually their growing child can bring his version of the way things are closer to the reality. Each time you read an Open Family Book and talk about it together, your child will take in what at that moment is most useful to him. Another day, another month, years later, other aspects of the book will be useful to him in quite different ways. The book will not have changed; what he needs, what he notices, how he uses it will change.

But that is what these books are for: to open between adult and child the potential for growth that exists in human beings of all ages.

This story is about divorce, though divorce does not actually take place. We have told the story this way because the reasons divorce is so shattering to children are clearer if we look at an intact family as a child sees it.

Inside this cardboard playhouse there is a mommy, a daddy and a baby. The baby cries a great deal, and is fed as often as a new-hatched robin. Mommy divides her time between dolling herself up, serving goodies and tidying. Daddy does important things marked by a great show of boots and toolbelts.

Such a stereotyped version of adult life has not been learned from these children's parents. Rather, children's play reflects their psychological perception of family roles and relationships.

Emotionally, there is only one baby—themselves. From that baby's point of view, a father is powerful, showy; a mother tends to pretty, homey needs.

All through this book a child's narrow view of family must be kept in mind. Were a child's feelings more easily separated from the facts, were his understanding and perception as complicated as ours, neither the threat nor the actuality of divorce would be so devastating.

Becky loves to play house with her friends. She is the baby. Heather and Tom are the mommy and daddy.

Children can't possibly play at ideas that have not occurred to them, and they don't waste energy on ones that don't concern them. Heather and Tom's parents are getting a divorce. Becky is learning for the first time that this can happen.

The first thing she learns from her friends is that "I don't like you anymore" can mean "I won't be married to you ever again." That piece of information can be taken in all too easily because it fits in the groove of childhood feelings. "I don't like her anymore," a child will say. "I'm never going to be her friend again."

If parents can leave one another because they don't like each other anymore, what will prevent them from walking out on an unlikable child? A child does not share our modern, adult view that marriage is a different, less organic bond than parenthood. When trust in one is broken, so is trust in the other.

"I don't like you anymore," the mommy tells the daddy. "I won't be married to you ever again. Here are your clothes. Go away."

The baby wants her daddy back. She cries and cries.

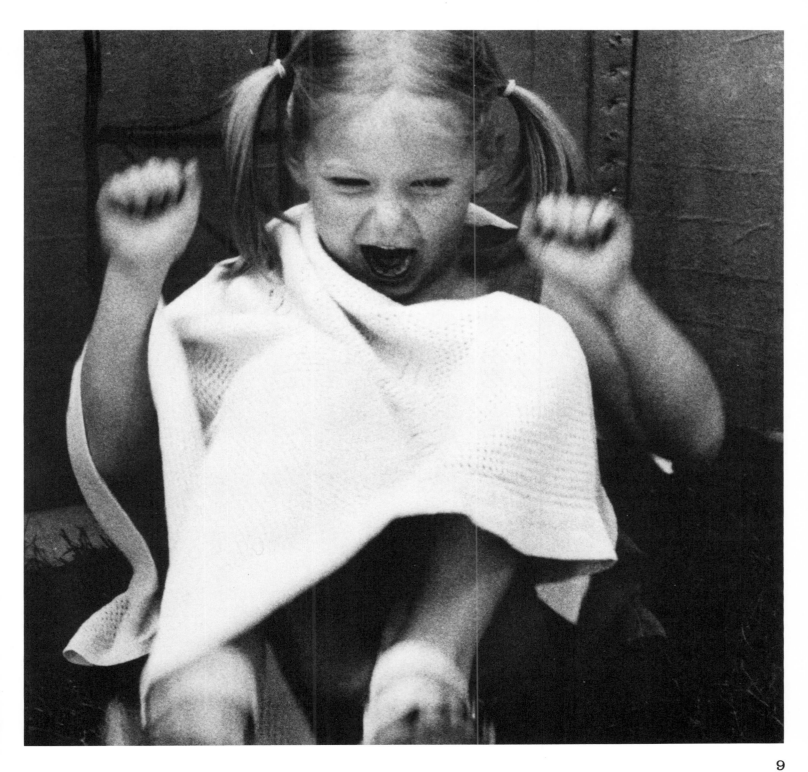

The reasons we give children for divorce are necessarily superficial. Even if we could articulate to ourselves the buried needs and wordless hurts that are the real cause, our children could not conceive of us as vulnerable, impotent, despairing or frightened. So we try to say what we feel is within their grasp: He takes the money, she bosses me around, we fight too much.

We are right, of course; this information is usable. It is also scary. All families have fights about these things. Every husband and wife yell, boss, criticize, cry. If this is how divorce happens, children might think, it could happen to anybody.

Playing house, like all imaginative play, is a method children use to work through problems. A child savors the pleasures of infancy to help himself put it truly behind him. He trades places with the doctor to help himself master the fact of being his patient. He steps into bigger shoes to try how he will manage when they really fit him. And he reenacts difficult events in bits and pieces to help himself take in the whole. All this is safe and good because it is "pretend."

When a child, like Becky now, precipitously leaves the game, it may be because the pretense hasn't worked. A threat has come too close, become too real. This game of divorce is too disturbing to continue.

Heather says Tom can't come back. He is too bossy. He yells too much. He has to be divorced.

Becky doesn't want to play with Heather and Tom anymore. She tells them to go home.

What has occurred to Becky is that her father might leave, might already be gone, might never come back. But she doesn't say that to her mother.

If children were to speak their minds, we would certainly have fewer problems raising them. We would understand immediately that a child won't take a bath because he is afraid he will be sucked down the drain, or insists on sleeping on the floor because there are bad dreams under the mattress. Then we could act directly to relieve the fear, and not waste ourselves in mindless hassling. But since children are as human as the rest of us, that is not to be.

We keep a great deal of ourselves to ourselves not only because we don't want others to know it, but because we don't want to know it either. We may feel enraged at someone, yet cannot shout "I hate you." The words would make it true, and make it permanent.

If Becky plays divorce without discussing divorce, if she asks where her father is instead of whether he has gone for good, she can protect herself from her worst fear. It may be hovering over the waters of her mind, but it is not yet the word.

"Where is Daddy?" Becky asks her mother at lunch. "He's at work, of course. Where did you think he was?"

When children of divorced families have been plumbed for their explanation, it comes out that they think they caused it. They wet their beds; desertion is the punishment. They got mad and wished Daddy would go away; the wish came true. Such ideas are incomprehensible until you realize how self-centered children's perceptions are, and how powerful they believe their thoughts to be.

When a toddler hides his eyes, he believes himself to be invisible. The only vision he can imagine is his own. A three-year-old can bite his mother in playful love, and fail to comprehend her reaction. He can feel his own feelings, not hers. Words and wishes have intrinsic force. "Bye bye," says the baby, not to mark his mother's leavetaking, but to create her disappearance while he smears the ointment. And even when this infant magician is nine or ten, his magic will not have entirely deserted him. There is a story about a schoolboy walking home, hitting each utility pole in turn with a stick. As he hit one pole, there was a blackout along the entire Eastern Seaboard. He thought he had done it. Causing a divorce would seem an easier magic.

"Where is Daddy?" Becky asks when the cartoons are over. "At work," her mother answers.

Not knowing what is on Becky's mind, her mother can't be very helpful. But she could offer more. She could, for instance, ask why Becky is so worried about where her daddy is, or reassure her that nothing has happened to him. Instead, she gets more and more irritated at this nagging question.

Maybe the question is nagging her too. We can imagine that this business of working late is a long-standing argument between her and her husband. We can imagine she isn't thrilled to eat supper with Becky, to do the dishes and the bedtime work alone, to retire to an empty bed, to think the thoughts wives think when husbands don't come home.

Parents have every right to be grumpy when things upset them.

But they must expect that their children will notice, think, feel and react. Her mother's irritation—and probably her anxiety as well—confirm Becky's nascent suspicions: Something is wrong.

"Where is Daddy?" Becky asks at suppertime. "Stop nagging!" her mother shouts. "He's working late again."

Daddy does not get home to give Becky a piggy-back ride to bed.

He does not get home to read her a bedtime story. He does not kiss her goodnight, or tuck her in, or turn her night light on.

19

When a baby is born, we inquire first as to its sex. If we didn't, we literally would not know what to do; because from that moment on we begin to speak, move, play and socialize with the infant according to its sex. We are chattier with baby girls, bouncier with baby boys. This is only the beginning of the process known as gender identity, whereby both mother and father respond to their child in a way that clarifies for him what sex he is, how that sex is perceived and how that sex is to behave.

By four or five, children, have already come a long way. They are in love, adept at courtship, and serious in their intention to marry their sweetheart. But a boy's sweetheart is his mommy, and a girl's is her daddy. Herein lies a normal crisis that is central to family life—and to divorce.

It occurs to children, as to any adult similarly in love, to do away with their rival—the other parent.

Then again, that won't do. A boy's sense of his own sex is rooted as much in his identification with his father as it is by contrast with his mother. In love with the one, he still loves and needs the other. For both boys and girls, the loss would be as terrifying as the gain seems blissful.

Not surprisingly, this time in a

child's life is punctuated by bad dreams. Those wishes, so passionately entertained, are payable in anxiety. To resolve the anxious conflict, each child must find a way to court the opposite sex with the approval of his own. But an absent father cannot be courted, and an angry mother cannot be approving. For Becky, and for every child, there will be bad nights like this when neither parent can help with her predicament.

Becky wakes up in the middle of the night. She thinks no one is there. She screams, "Daddy, Daddy"

But Daddy is still not home.

We all know the less than innocent remarks husbands and wives make to one another when they are annoyed. You can recognize Becky's mother—fed up with her husband's coming home late, tired of so much work and no one to talk to; wondering if he really is working, if he really does love her; remembering how long it has been since he took her out; reviewing old injuries; dwelling on injustices—until out it comes, a swipe at him, a pointed mention of divorce. Not theirs of course. Somebody else's. The divorce next door.

But the message is clear. And Becky can hear every bit as well as her father can.

In the morning, there is Daddy. "Darling," says Becky's mother. "Did you hear about Heather and Tom? Their parents are getting a divorce."

"Hmm," says Becky's father. "They seemed happy to me."

"That's because you're never home to hear
them fighting," Becky's mother says.

Becky can act like a woman too. Interrupting her rival, she sidles over to her daddy, drapes herself against him, and with barely masked seduction pleads for the gift a husband gives his wife: a baby.

A "real" baby, one that eats and cries. Dear Daddy, a foolish Adam falling for the apple.

Should he have? No, not quite so hard at least. He could have said, "That sounds like a good idea, but right now I'm talking to Mommy." Steering a more moderate course during a moment of tension would have been helpful to Becky. It would have hinted that he looked warmly upon Becky's courtship, but was married to someone else. There are times the most charming of daughters needs to see that Mommy might come first.

Becky interrupts. She wants Daddy to give her a real baby doll that eats and cries. Daddy says yes.

We may all have spoken words similar to these dozens of times. The words, however, are not the argument. To buy or not to buy a doll, to go to work, to stay home—no, not cause enough for such strong feelings, for such pain that it could someday really lead to divorce.

Unexpressed, unmet—sometimes inexpressible and unmeetable—needs burst forth in anger on the barest of occasions.

Yet to ask that our deepest needs be met is to be vulnerable. We might be refused. Anticipating rejection in advance, a step is skipped. No tears precede the anger. No one says what they really mean, or really want. They hide their hurt behind the hassle.

Becky can't be expected to see more than her parents can see, to realize buried pains, old disappointments, earlier needs carried perhaps from childhoods of their own. All she can see is the anger. And it is big. As big as hers is sometimes. Maybe as uncontrollable. Maybe as vicious. They could hurt each other.

And whose fault is this scary thing? What started it? In antagonism to her mother, in seduction of her father, Becky asked for a baby. No wonder she doesn't want to hear, doesn't want to see, must run away.

"Now wait a second," says
Becky's mother.
"Don't think you can work late all
the time and then make
everything all right with a present."
"I can buy Becky anything I
want!" yells Daddy.
"How come you can do anything
you want and I have to
stay home and take care of
everything!" her mommy yells back.

Becky thinks Daddy
will hit Mommy.

Is it a bad thing to have a fight in front of children? No. This story is not a plea to conduct anger in whispers behind locked doors "for the children's sake." It is a plea to deal with the results. After the battle—and certainly before a separation or divorce—it is the obligation of parents to call a truce and take the time to see to the needs of their children.

They stop fighting.
Becky is gone.
They don't know where she is.

145619

CODY MEMORIAL LIBRARY
SOUTHWESTERN UNIVERSITY
GEORGETOWN, TEXAS

31

A child's needs, logical though they might be, are not often clear to us. Becky's mother didn't see a connection between her own irritation the night before and her daughter's trouble sleeping; or between Becky's persistent nagging and the divorce next door. Her father didn't see the seduction in her plea for a baby, nor the uneasiness his promise aroused.

If these are mistakes, they are entirely innocent. We all must make them. In fact, if we were mind readers, we would upset our children even more. Only once in a while can a child make things come as clear to us as Becky does now. She asks outright if her parents are getting a divorce.

The question is not easy to answer. Nearly half our marriages end in divorce, and of these a great many involve families with young children. For those under seven or eight, the prognosis for their later emotional health—unless their problems are understood and dealt with—may be worse than if one parent had died.

Becky is asking a very serious question.

# "Are you getting a divorce?" Becky asks.

Becky's parents can give a truthful answer for now. No, a fight is not a divorce. In fact, though they, like any of us, have thought of living apart at times, Becky's fear may help them think again. Faced with the seriousness of a child's view of marriage, the word "split" appalls us with its casualness. Divorce is not coffee time gossip, or cocktail party news. It is not a pat solution to "lack of communication," or an "identity crisis." It is not even "liberation." Divorce is a family catastrophe. Becky's parents see it for a moment. There is only one way to consider a divorce: with full awareness of just how much it hurts husband, wife and children.

"No, we are not getting a divorce."

Anger is a strange emotion. It so often looks different on the outside from the way it feels inside. We yank a child from the street, and scream at him in fury while our hearts race in fear. We are sarcastic to a husband who has forgotten an anniversary while our hearts sink in disappointment. We yell and lash out, and know that if only someone would hug us, we could cry.

This is what we must say to children, in simple ways like Becky's parents are saying now. Anger is not the opposite of love. We are most bitter with those to whom we are most attached, from whom we need the most, with whom we have shared the most. It is not the least bit strange that from the distance of time, the most awful of family fights may become the happiest of family jokes.

"You know I shout at you, and still love you," says her father. "You know I get mad at you and still take care of you," says her mother.

"And we can have a fight
today, and still be married."

Were we able to watch Becky and Heather and Tom play "divorce" for longer, we might see in comic parody our own attempts to comfort and justify ourselves. Will Tom put down Heather's ability to dress their child properly? Will Heather complain about late payments, or remark about Tom's girl friend? Maybe watching such a soap opera as replayed by children would help us see how sad divorce really is, how stripped of fatherhood a father, how lonely his wife, how confused the children.

Then what do you do about all the things you want to complain about? You don't really have to say, "Daddy never talks to me," when you could say, "I need a man who will talk to me." Complaints are better saved for the ears of friends, and for a simple reason. A child has only one mommy, one daddy. That either one was right, or wrong, victim or victimizer cannot change his need to be like the one, and in love with the other. Insult and recrimination, severe restrictions in visiting, too early an intrusion of a "new" parent, interfere terribly with his own relationships. A child does not love either parent less because they love each other less. Both of you will still take care of your baby.

After that day, Heather and Tom still come over to play house. Sometimes they play being married. They all live in the same house. Sometimes they play being divorced. The mommy and daddy live in different houses.

But they always take care of their baby.

Adults may not realize in advance how at a loss they will feel after a divorce. It is as if, after so many years of marriage, they no longer know themselves without it. Turning to a child as a stand-in for a spouse is not at all uncommon.

Though standing in for an adult may seem to be the realization of a secret dream, it is paid for dearly in guilt. What children need is to flirt with the idea of stealing one parent from the other, to be allowed to toy with it playfully, so that in the end they can give it up as an impossible dream and get on with the business of growing up.

Becky's father could fall into the same pattern separated husbands do. He still comes home late. No doubt his wife is no more pleasant about it than she was a few weeks earlier. Becky, in the knowing way of children, may intrude herself into this gap, feeling out a woman's feelings towards a man, finding where she fits. And he could respond, finding in a four-year-old an easy admiration. But this man is husband to his wife, father to his child. The two presents he brings home—peace offerings though they may be—will show he clearly knows the difference.

After that day, Becky's father still comes home late from work. One night he has two presents with him.

Becky gets a baby doll, but it is a simple one who neither eats nor cries. She is not at all "real." There is a gentle rebuff here. Daddy is not Becky's husband, not the man who will someday give her a real baby. He is a father who can only give a doll.

For the woman he married, the present is of another sort altogether: a gown, an evening out, a time to be together all by themselves.

Parents might hesitate to flaunt their relationship just when their daughter so openly courts her father, so openly challenges her mother. Not at all. This is exactly the reassurance Becky needs. Much as Daddy loves her, he will not let Becky stand between his wife and him. She is not that powerful. She will not be able to get rid of her mother. The wish is a plaything; it cannot come to life. Becky can love her father, and keep her mother too.

Children in separated families need to know the same thing. They no more had the power to cause the separation than they have now to be a parent's mate. Playing is allowed to children. But only grown-ups can consummate their love, or bring about its dissolution.

A baby doll for Becky. A beautiful dress for Mommy.

While she awaits adulthood and all the pleasures and powers she thinks will then be hers, this little girl is beginning to step beyond the limits of her earlier vision. Tomorrow, perhaps, she will wrap herself in that perfumed velvet cape, and breathe in her mother's pleasure. The cape, the perfume, the feelings are not her own. They are her mother's. Over the next few years she will try on the feelings, thoughts and visions of many other people, until she can cry for another's pain, read another's thoughts, see through another's eyes.

No one will ever, forever, be able to answer Becky's question about divorce. All we can hope is that, married or divorced, if we can raise a child in such a way that he can resolve his own predicaments, he will grow up to understand ours.

"While Becky takes care of her baby," says Daddy, "I'm going to take care of my wife."

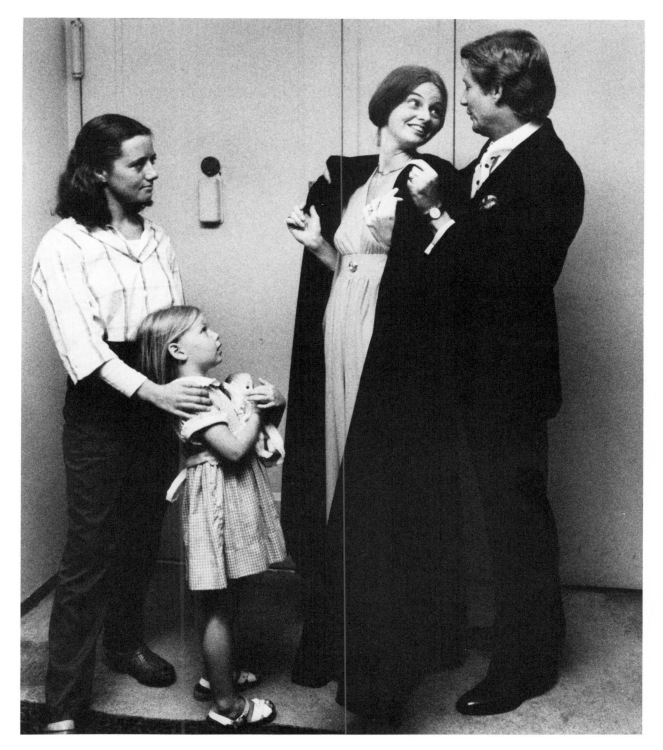

"After all, I wouldn't want
her to divorce me."